BEYOND MY NEEDS

A NEW BOOK BY
MARVA SIMON

Learning to compromise and how it saved my marriage.

Bloomington, IN   Milton Keynes, UK

AuthorHouse™
1663 Liberty Drive,
Suite 200
Bloomington, IN 47403
www.authorhouse.com
Phone: 1-800-839-8640

AuthorHouse™ UK Ltd.
500 Avebury Boulevard
Central Milton Keynes,
MK9 2BE
www.authorhouse.co.uk
Phone: 08001974150

First published by AuthorHouse 4/09/2007

ISBN: 978-1-4343-0846-7

Printed in the United States of America
Bloomington, Indiana

This book is printed on acid-free paper.

Book Design:
Creative Director: Adriannie Morgan-Webbe
Graphic Designer: Vivian Sánchez

Gana Gana Land Advertising & Design, Inc.
8232 NW 8th Place
Plantation, FL 33324
Phone: 954-452-0441
www.ganaganaland.com

ACKNOWLEDGMENTS

No one ever writes a book on their own; I could not have done this without God and the ideas and motivation of others.

I acknowledge the gift given to me by God and his inspiration to write this book. My gratitude to him is not enough to write with pen and paper. I thank him for the professional advice, books and teaching materials gathered through preachers from various organizations.

To my husband, Leslie,
Thank you – for putting up with me while I am preoccupied with writing. The years have really flown by, since we fell in love, and they have brought me new reasons to love you more. You have been my lover, my friend and partner for more than twenty years. You have been strong when I needed to lean on you. You have been there when I needed you to listen and understand. Even though I did not realize it until later and don't always remember to tell you how much I love and appreciate you, you are still the one who makes my heart beat faster. You are the one I will always love. I am really privileged to stand by your side as a helpmate. As God has commissioned us, may our lives continue to be a light that shines as an example; so others may see God through us. Thanks be to God for giving you to me in such a time as this.

To our sons Marlon, Craig, Brian and Christopher,
You were entrusted to us by God and you are the "apples of my eyes." I love and appreciate you all and also want you to know how important you are in my life. God could not have given me a better set of boys for which to care. You are the best among the rest. To God be the glory for the things he has done!

To my son Craig,
I am indebted to you for playing the part of "marriage counselor," when I had slipped into one of my worst mood-swings regarding your father. I cannot calculate my gratitude for that special Friday evening session. You have made the difference in our lives.

To my beloved mother, Clara G. Chambers,
Thank you for your influence. You taught me how to persevere in struggle and to survive with little. You taught me to keep on going for the sake of my children.

To my sister, Patricia Hall,
You always have faith in me and your encouragement has helped me along.

To my niece, Michelle,
If you continue writing at your age and speed, girl, you will make it.

To my sister-in-law, Blossom Simon,
I believe when sisters-in-law were first originated, you were selected from one of the best seeds. Thank you for your love and support. It really means a lot.

To my dear sister-in-Christ, Morvett Carter,
You are a blessing. Your encouragement played a big role in this project. God bless you for your help, love and support.

To Adriannie Morgan-Webbe and Vivian Sánchez,
You are responsible for making this a reality.

CONTENTS

INTRODUCTION

When my husband and I married, I expected life to be perfect; just like the wedded bliss portrayed by Hollywood. I have always been a dreamer and a romantic. And our courtship was nothing less than made for the movies; we quickly fell deeply in love and, oh, so romantically. I expected all the initial euphoria to last the rest of our lives.

Unfortunately, my naive expectations were quickly marred by reality. I did not adjust to the changes of married life very well. Instead of seeing the beauty in what we had, I longed for a never-ending "fairy tale." Looking back, I did not have a clue about what marriage was really about. Back then, I felt severely shortchanged; I thought my marriage was a failure. Unknowingly, I was holding up my Godly union to completely unrealistic standards. I needed to change my vision but it took a long time for me to hear, accept and trust God's guidance.

Even worse, it took me longer to realize that I was far from being the only one who faced such issues. So many people get married in ignorance. I think the majority of couples are in the dark when they marry. We do not know the sacrifice, surprises, commitment, endurance, compromise, love and so much more that it takes to keep up a marriage. We ought to know that every relationship has its ups and downs. We have to fight and be brave against all evil and never run away. With knowledge we can prepare ourselves for the journey.

Leslie and I were destined to be together, yet we went through many unnecessarily difficult times. Our joy in companionship was delayed because of my ignorance about marriage. I am so grateful we made it through but so many people do not.

For those of you struggling, the joys are worth all the hard times. Learning to live with and love one another, as God intended, becomes a wonderful gift, far greater than any previous expectation.

If, by my experience, I can make a difference in one person's life and marriage, it'll be worth the difficulty in learning these lessons.

FROM TURKEY WINGS TO WEDDING RING
Chapter 1

At that first kiss, cold reason stood aside,
With folded arms to let a grand love
Enter into my soul's secret chamber to abide.
With sincerity I prayed to God,
My great high priest, my first love and my last.
There on His altar, I consumed my past,
And all my life, I lay upon its shrine;
The best emotions of my heart and brain,
Whatever gifts and graces may be mine.
No secrets, thoughts, no memory I can retain
But give them all for dear love's precious sake.
Complete surrender of the whole I made.
"Lord, I speak unafraid what I know to be true.
This fire, this flame that burns inside
Like sweet incense for him,
What had he done to my heart?
If you are the cause for all this, Lord then let it be.
Dear Lord, please let it be."

It was a chilly, Friday evening, July 10, 1983; the church was open in preparation for the church's Annual Soul-Winning Movie. It was approximately 6:45 p.m. The movie was scheduled to start at seven but by then it was already a full house. "I'll get it," said the thirty-one year-old gentleman, who was well built like a hunk and sporting a jet-black moustache. He maneuvered his way through the inner court of the Tabernacle of Prayer, passing a number of believers conversing, to let me in.

As I entered through the glass doors from the cold, with my hands in the pockets of my spring jacket, I glanced nervously at this handsome man holding the door; and then at the man standing next to him, who also appeared to be very friendly. They both ushered me through the aisles and we all sat together for the movie. We introduced ourselves and had a brief conversation before the movie started. The man who had opened the door, his name was Leslie Simon. We were both new to the church and realized we were both from Jamaica. I met a few more church members that night and I exchanged phone numbers with some. Even though Leslie was one of them, the memory of that evening had slipped my mind.

It was only a few days later I recalled seeing him, when we met up again in the new members meeting. Pastor Johnnie Washington asked all new members to stand up and introduce themselves.

"My name is Brother Leslie Simon, and I am here for the first time," he said. My eyes were wide open.

"I know this guy," I said to myself, remembering him from the movie night.

My eyes focused on him as he continued speaking. I could not say for what reason. However, as he took his seat, I kept thinking there was no doubt of a divine connection between this man and myself.

He surprised me with a phone call three weeks later. The phone rang four times.

"Hello," he said.
"Hello," I replied.
"Hello," he repeated.
"How are you?" he asked.

"I am fine," I said but I was lying like a dog. How could I say I was fine when I was shaking like a leaf hanging on its branch? I tried to control myself. I did not want him to get a clue of my nervousness. However, we managed to speak for quite a while. We spoke about general things; Jamaica, how we ended up at that church, et cetera. We seemed to really connect and by the time the long conversation was over, I knew the two of us were no longer strangers.

With confidence and without hesitation I asked, "Do you like turkey wings? This is an invitation for dinner." I suppose his response was yes; I did not wait to hear the exact words. I told him dinner would be served at seven the next evening and we said goodbye. I wanted to get to know him better, in person. But the only thing I had in my refrigerator to prepare were some old, bony, turkey wings. I hoped to myself that, maybe, he wouldn't mind turkey wings.

Anxiously, I waited for the next day to come. Feeling like a child on Christmas morning, I wanted the evening to be romantic but had forgotten to purchase candles. However, my fast-thinking self turned off the lights in the kitchen and left the hallway lights on, so it would look romantic. I wanted this evening to be a successful one. I made sure everything was well prepared, especially the wings. I did not want anything to mess up this date.

Again, the conversation went effortlessly. We talked about our likes and dislikes and found out we had a lot in common. We spoke about our faith. I told him about my values and my expectations of a man. He told me about his values and his wants in a woman. He seemed advanced in his faith, which I admired. We spoke about our families and pretty much every possible topic. All evening he was a gentleman. The whole thing went beautifully; it seemed like my very first date.

When he gave me a light kiss on my lips and complimented me on dinner, it felt as if it was the first kiss I had ever received in my life. I liked it and wished he would never stop.

Not long after, he called to say he made it home safely. Before I hung up, he paused for a moment and I wondered what was going on. After a while, he spoke in a tone of voice I had never heard before.

"Will you marry me?" he said.
"What?!" I said incredulously.
"You heard me," he replied.

I was stunned. I thought to myself this was just a joke. I was laughing so hard I could have died. I hardly knew this man. Where did he get off asking me this kind of a question? It was just one date. Did he realize what he was saying? How could a man propose to a woman in such a short period of time? It had only been three weeks since we saw each other for the first time. The questions kept rushing through my mind and he must have realized my reluctance to answer.

"Okay, you don't have to give me an answer now. I'll meet with you tomorrow and we'll talk more about it."

"Okay," I said and we hung up the phone.

For the entire night I was in a state of shock. There were a million and one things going through my mind. Once again I found it hard to sleep.

Luckily, it was the weekend. I consoled myself that I had cooked him such sweet turkey wings. They were nothing but bones and poultry, yet they caused a man to sweep a woman off her feet and for him to propose to her in no time.

When Leslie proposed marriage to me, I wondered what he wanted from me. Neither of us had anything to offer each other, we hardly knew each other. I did not know where he got the idea of marriage so suddenly. I only knew with that first phone call something inside of me had connected to this man I hardly knew. It was so strange.

I wasn't sure if I was ready to make a commitment to Leslie or any other man, the entire situation seemed to be out of place. I needed to get my act together and focus on the Lord. I had failed him too much and wanted to come back home where I belonged. I knew the Lord had a plan for my life and so I was ready for God's will to occur in my life. But marriage was definitely not what I had in mind at that time.

> *"He reveals deep and secret things; He knows what is in the darkness and light dwells with Him." (Danile 2:22)*

I began to ask myself questions and as the questions mounted, answers were also popping up. Somehow it began to make sense to me that this was the purpose and will of God. This was the reason why the Lord had spoken to me and told me to go the Tabernacle House of Prayer. It was a set-up; the Lord had planned the meeting between Leslie and me without our knowledge. Even though I smiled at the fix up between Leslie and me – I noticed that God did not give me what I really "wanted." I always liked my men six foot tall and around 235 pounds; Leslie was five foot four inches and about 150 pounds. I realized that God does not give us what we think we want; he gives us what's best for us.

Few things happen in life as pure coincidence; major events are usually preceded by sequences of smaller, seemingly unrelated occurrences. Old folks used to call it the "handwriting on the wall." Too often we ignore the handwriting on the wall, even when it is so bright and in bold letters.

No event or situation occurs without purpose. God always knows what is best; despite what we think we want or need. The handwriting on the wall presents itself to give us an opportunity to complete its message. It is a clue or a heads-up on what is to come. It warrants investigation and exploration, so that we may learn the purpose of the lesson being presented. Don't judge or ignore it. Use the power of spiritual discernment to reveal that which is not obvious to the five senses. The wisdom we find in praying and meditation can then guide us, correctly, in taking our next set of steps.

THE HONEYMOON BEGINS
Chapter 2

Marriage, at first, was a God-like separate existence.
Our world was set apart in some fair clime.
I had no will, purpose, or resistance.
The earth seemed something foreign and afar
And we were two sovereigns dwelling in a star.
I almost doubt that all these years could be
Before we met, that we had any part in life until
We clasped each other with love enraptured thrill.

On Monday, November 14, 1983, dressed in casual apparel Leslie and I made our way to downtown Manhattan, New York and were joined in marriage. We were on a final runway to a commitment that would last a lifetime. My sister Patricia accompanied us as a witness at our marriage that day. We arrived at the court house about 10:00 a.m. that morning. By the time we got married it was almost noon. On our way back home from the wedding, we thought it would be nice to sit down and have a nice lunch at one of our favorite restaurants in Queens. It was about 12:30 p.m. in the afternoon by then. It was indeed a wonderful afternoon, as we laughed, talked and celebrated this special occasion.

My sister Patricia was such a character, a drama queen. She had us in stitches from laughing so much. At one point I almost choked on a piece of meat. The day was a successful and joyful one; I fulfilled my need of being a married woman.

I could not believe that I was actually married, I felt Leslie's hand holding onto me. I almost jumped him, but then I looked on my finger and realized that he was actually my husband.

Each day of our new marriage brought about new meaning in our lives as we shared our lives and our love for each other. During this period we refused to turn our backs from each others needs. We were so devoted to each other. Like most other newlywed couples, we could not keep our hands off each other. We found each other irresistible. On the street people would just look at us and see the love we exuded.

It was three months after the wedding that we found out I was with child. When Marlon, our first son, was born, our love grew even stronger. We were the two happiest people that ever lived on the face of this earth. We continued to go to church together, shared in church activities and with family, and watched our little boy grow. Looking back, there were slight indications of problems to come but we were focused on our family and our good fortune.

By the time Craig, our second child was born, it seemed as if it was the first time giving birth. Then along came Brian and Christopher, our third and fourth boys. Leslie was a great caregiver during my pregnancies; he would cook me the best chicken soup when I was unable to keep anything else down. His soup was the only thing my nauseated stomach would tolerate.

Leslie was such a proud father and man of God. When each of the boys were born and we brought them home from the hospital, he placed each of them on the bed and said to them, "This is the place where you were conceived, and I am offering you back to the Lord."

My family was wonderful. I loved being a mother; I loved my husband and my children so much. We lived in New York and did not have a car for some time. As a family, we would walk quite a distance to church; we had some fun times walking. I have wonderful memories of one or two of the boys pushing their brother in the carriage and I was pregnant with another. It was a joyous experience watching the boys running, playing and dancing on the way.

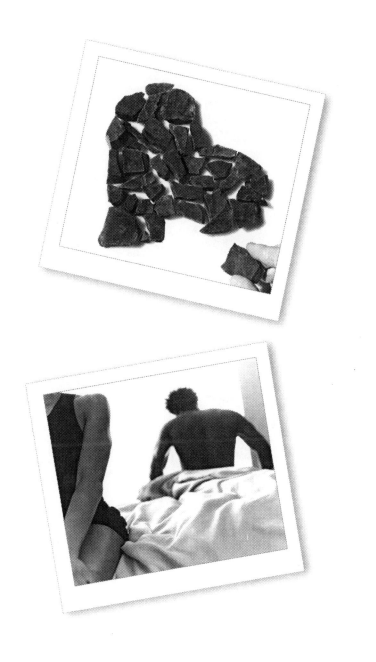

THE HONEYMOON ENDS
Chapter 3

Words may be mild and fair.
Words may be soft as the summer air,
But one may break the heart.
Words come forth from the mind.
The tone leaps from the inner self,
Revealing the state of the heart.

Negative feelings mixed in with the excitement of being a new wife and mother. Although I loved my husband and my children, all sorts of emotions were taking over. My body had not handled pregnancy and childbearing too well. Each pregnancy was more difficult and made me ill. After each birth, I would have to stay in the hospital longer than normal.

Each pregnancy also brought mounting feelings of loneliness. I became sad and confused. I felt so inexperienced, not knowing what a marriage and family entailed. My head was inundated with more questions than I had answers for. Something in me was out of balance. Nowadays, I would have been diagnosed with post-partum depression but back then we had no knowledge of this syndrome.

With a sweet and caring husband and beautiful boys, I could not comprehend the contrast in my emotions. Leslie was a loving and caring husband, yet I became increasingly irritable and demanding of him. To say I was cranky would be an understatement. The behavior continued and increased beyond the childbearing years.

Something in me longed for the fairytale life. Where were the constant flowers, showering of love and kisses, the massages and trips at the spur of the moment? Where was the passion, the fun and excitement? With both of us working and taking care of the boys, we were tired, with little time for each other. When did I sign up for this? This is not what I envisioned for my marriage. Oddly enough, the moments we did have together, I was reacting towards him in such a way, he could not touch me. As months, then years passed, I ignored him more and absorbed myself more in motherhood than being a wife.

Not surprisingly, sometimes I felt I lived with a stranger. There were days I would barely say hello. Whenever I did speak to Leslie, I was loud and belligerent. I used words inappropriately to make him feel insignificant. My words sometimes turned into threats of leaving and divorcing him.

Everything he did or did not do I took offensively and personaly. Nothing he did pleased me. Personal habits irritated me. I would use any little thing to start a big argument.

There were times he would drive my car and leave the gas tank on empty. Oh, how that would aggravate me. He might not have realized it as he was racing home to make up for lost time or rushing home to change for a church meeting. "You are so thoughtless! You better go back and fill my tank up!" I would demand.

Sometimes he missed a birthday or our anniversary. Such forgetfulness fueled my anger and made me go behind his back and do mean things out of spite. Revenge persisted longer than necessary, out of a growing anger. When he realized his mistakes, he was so apologetic, so concerned. I did not care one bit how he felt. Yet, I constantly accused him of being the one who did not care about me. I thought he wasn't doing enough. I felt he didn't cater to me enough; I expected him to treat me like a queen no matter my action... His regret did not matter, only my self-justification. I could have cared less about how he felt. Honestly, I didn't even know what I really wanted, I just felt shortchanged.

Caught up in selfishness, I did not see when Leslie became tired of my behavior or how he suffered for my disillusionment in the marriage. During the early years, for the most part, he would not complain. Later on, he thought I was trying to control him. Eventually, he refused to given a damn. All of his attempts to ease me failed, so why bother trying at all. He became increasingly sarcastic and cynical. The sarcasm would just dig under my skin. "Who does he think he is?" Our marriage was like a bowling ball rolling down the track.

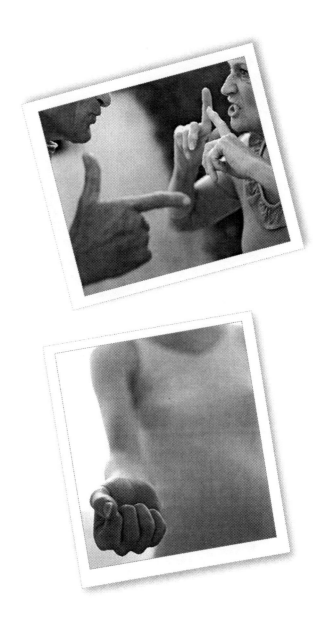

"UNDER MY DEAD BODY"
Chapter 4

Positive words are good,
But false words should not be uttered.

I had an eye-opening experience watching an elderly couple almost throw punches at each other in a retirement community where I was working at the time. Storming down the stairs from the second floor, I saw an elderly man in his seventies or eighties, along with his wife marching behind him. I soon realized the two had argued while playing a poker game with their neighbor upstairs. The man was in a temper so uncontrollable that he could have had a heart attack.

"You son-of-a-b****, I don't care if your lips touch your chin, you can talk as long as you want; I'll never say I'm sorry even 'til 'thy kingdom comes!'" he shouted violently. "And I don't care either you bastard, I'll never forgive you under my dead body for what you did to me," said the elderly woman. "These two are always at it," added one nosy neighbor. "You would think that after fifty-five years of marriage they would have learned to stop fighting," said another neighbor.

It was then I wondered to myself, how could they have survived for so long under these conditions? Their rage, anger, bickering, and lack of forgiveness had led up to this hate. How could two people live like this?

Even when death knocks at our doors, God's mercy still endures, but if 'under our dead bodies' we cannot forgive, then where will we spend eternity?

I thought about my own marriage and saw Leslie and me in that couple. The anger that woman expressed was the anger I had as well. Was this the future for us? No! I thought. If life has any meaning or value at all, I shouldn't allow my relationship to end up this way. There is a life beyond this one and to continue in this manner would destroy us and our family.

Upon retrospection, I know watching that couple was the first turning point. Still, after the experience, the anger and bitterness would not fade. It spread; I wasn't just angry with Leslie but also with myself. I was angry at myself for behaving the way I had for so long; I was angry for constantly being angry at my husband, I was angry because I was still bitter and could not stop myself from the disrespectful behaviors. I tried to hold on to good but evil presented itself. Every time I blew up at Leslie, I would feel justified in the moment. Then I would feel so guilty later for the way I treated him. The devil was having his way in my thoughts, in my actions and in our lives.

TAKING LOVE FOR GRANTED
Chapter 5

Through the many changing years,
we've lived and loved together
Through good times and bad,
we've shared each other's gladness
And wept each other's tears;
but often times we forget.
The sorrow, I never knew
that was long unsuited by thee.
We've played with each other's emotions,
and have taken too lightly

The value of the goodness each other possess;
The smiles we've shared produced a summer
Where darkness else would be.
Like the leaves that fall
around us in autumn's fading hours
Are traitor's smiles that darken
when the cloud of sorrow lowers;
And though many such we've known,
Love, too prone, alas, to range.

The wind tossed me about and I was driven by the unrealistic character that plagued my mind, to become someone other than my true self. It was so difficult to hold on to sensitivity and to even maintain the passion so vital to a relationship. I allowed it to dissipate in such ways and allowed aggravation to take over with such force; it was difficult for me to establish the appropriate behavior as a wife and mother.

My harsh words were a reflection of my discontent. Whether I had known it or not, whether I had meant it or not, there are so many negative words that I had spoken that could have been avoided. Unfortunately, the harm had already been done.

Though I tried to think positively, my attitude took the best of me, and damaged my spiritual commitment with the Lord. I could have prevented the irritability and implemented a positive attitude in regards to the many good deeds done for me, yet I found myself taken everything for granted. I allowed the anger and bitterness to override and set myself swinging from mood swing to mood swing. It launched me into depression with folded arms, withdrawn and letting the nasty virus of self-pity to take control; using me to behave childishly. In a manner as to let me ignore the one who had my best interest at heart, and for me to turn appreciation into ungratefulness upon my mate.

Guilt consumed me. How could I act like this? My husband had married a saved woman. What happened to her he probably could not fathom. I wonder what kind of person, a Christian, a 'born again' believer, does the things I did? As my actions toward Leslie came more in perspective, I beat myself up more and more. How could he survive such a relationship? Yes, I feel bad for my actions, I keep saying I will change but my attitude is the same. I felt I had no willpower; I was incapable of being the wife Leslie deserved.

The more time passed the worse I felt, I felt like a horrible person. All the choices I made seemed wrong. At times, I wondered if I was just being melodramatic. Were the problems all in my head?

The devil convinced me it was all just a big lie to begin with. Why did we even bother to get married?

THE TURNAROUND
Chapter 6

It is not so much to seek
To be consoled
As to console,
Or to be understood
As to understand
Or to be loved
As to love.

After years of making my husband and myself miserable, I turned thoughts of leaving Leslie into a concrete plan. The void in our marriage seemed immense. We had been married over twenty years. Most of those years were in struggle; why keep each other in torment any longer? I could not fathom spending the rest of our lives like that old couple. Divorce was a horrible thought and I was terrified of all the possible outcomes. Yet, the problems were still there and I was more afraid the issues would get bigger and more destructive.

With a tormented mind, I told my boys about my plans to leave their father. It was a Friday evening, November 18, 2000, and I was driving them to a school meeting. Their reactions jolted me. They knew our marriage had problems but divorce was far beyond what they imagined. Their sadness, devastation, and the threat of one of them running away was more pain than I had anticipated. They launched out an attack of bewilderment and melancholy towards me. They were all expressing their feelings to me, trying to convince me to stay with their father.

After they were through talking and giving me words of encouragement, I then realized that it was not a good idea for me to file for a divorce. I could see the sorrow in their little faces. I wondered what I would put my children through, for them to see their parents that they love so much get a divorce.

Seeing them in that state and listening to them changed something in me. The experience allowed me to see what is most important in my life. I realized how I act and how truly it affected others around me. My role and feelings as a wife extended greatly into my role as a mother. The guilt was unbearable, how could I have been so consumed in just my feelings? Clearly, I had to pick up the pieces and make the impossible become possible. If our children, who were the most innocent in all of this, could be assured a future with both parents, should I not make a real effort to go the extra mile?

I had continued to play the role of not only a mother but a wife as well. I had to bring about a change in my relationship with a positive attitude; stay focused, and allow God's likeness and glory to be seen in me.

PRAYER
Chapter 7

Whatever it is, its best I will be
Under each rank; wrong sometimes,
lies the root of right.
Each sorrow has its purpose,
by the sorrowing of the inquest;
But as sure as the sun brings morning
I know that each sinful action will not go unpunished,
As sure as the night brings shade,
It is somewhere, sometimes, the fact we can't derive.
Though the hour be long delayed,
I know that the soul is aided
sometimes by the heart's unrest,
And to grow means often to suffer.
Nevertheless, what ever it is, its best I will be.
There are no errors in the great eternal plan,
And all things work together for the final good of man.
I know when my soul speeds
onward in its grand eternal quest,
I shall say as I look back earthward,
Earth has no sorrow that heaven cannot heal.
So what ever it is, its best I will be.

After the conversation with my children, I forced myself to stop and think about how I had allowed my negative feelings to get the better of our marriage and me. I did not really want my marriage to end; I just wanted things to be better. I thought long and hard, and prayed even harder.

"The instrument of thy peace, oh Lord. Where there is hatred, please let me show love. If injured, doubtful, or lacking faith in despair, even when you had promised you would have taken me through, Lord, I beg your pardon. In humility, I bow as my soul rejoices deep down. I can still feel the fear lingering but unto thee, O Lord, I give myself that thou will keep and guide me. All that seemed over, let it once again be rejuvenated. Today the blessing you impart has renewed my faith and has directed my path anew. The things you would have me to do, give me the patience that I need just for today. All other troubles, I leave to thee for tomorrow."

Before long, prayer brought me numerous realizations. God first let me know I would have to look way inside of me and prepare to work hard. I would have to entrust my marriage to him wholeheartedly, pray and ask for his guidance constantly. By doing that, I could start turning things around.

It was a difficult road. First were the insights to the mistakes I had made over the years. I would have to think about, pray about, analyze, and forgive myself for each of them. God also instructed me not to beat myself up for them any longer; no more self-pity, the devil would not win.

I had done a lot of criticizing and little to really fix things. Unconsciously, I had put Leslie in charge of the entire marriage. I blamed him for all that was wrong and waited around expecting him to be the one to change and change things. I also had to stop behaving like a martyr and acknowledge Leslie did not know the extent of my unhappiness. I had failed to communicate years of shifting emotions and disappointments with him. I had been in my own world of thoughts and silent accusations. How could he have possibly tried to address some of those concerns? He could not read my mind to know all my frustrations; he just saw a nagging, dissatisfied wife.

More of my mistakes would enter my head. Accusing him of not loving me, not keeping his promises and more, were way out of line. I had not been accepting of him, had tried to dominate and

change him. I also had harbored years of small wrongs he had done, stored in my memory, which I needed to let go. It was difficult to admit I had been unfair to my husband. I had to accept the things I could not change, change the things that I could, and ask God for the wisdom to distinguish one from the other.

"But, why Lord, had I been so angry and bitter?"

More answers were given to me.

As a young child, my father had left my mother and me. The one man that I thought loved me unconditionally, broke that trust and my heart. He told me he loved me and I cherished the feeling.

But he left, without notice and it would be years before I saw him again. The devastation and resentment of my father leaving had festered in me. Unknowingly, I had great difficulty trusting a man's love. Being unable to forgive had taken a toll on my heart, wielding its unholy influence in my life. A heavy load of emotions, none of them good, took over. Emotions of love, security and fraternity were replaced by feelings of hurt, anguish and pains of the past.

I arrived at the place of conflict and contention, quite unintentionally. Leslie paid in many ways for my father's actions and my unforgivingness. The distrust in a man's love caused me to constantly doubt Leslie's words and criticize his effort.

Getting beyond that point posed the difficulty. Once we humans suffer an unfairness or injustice, we often develop what I call "a cage of protective unforgivingness," as happened with me. We tell ourselves "no one will ever hurt me again." To ensure that, we build a defense system that allows only limited outside access. An emotional barricade surrounds us as a relational fortress, protecting us from future harm. We decide that nothing is going to get in again and repeat the trauma we have endured. When this protective wall has been erected, no one gets in, and regrettably, nothing gets out either. Because of this anxiety mounts, pressure builds, bitterness grows, hate and anger develop. These influences intrude into all other areas of our spirit and drown it to the point of no return. For me it became so easy to become cynical and critical of Leslie. When these things took hold, I became an easy target for depression as feelings of isolation set in. Unforgivingness is the offspring of the devil. He is a liar a thief and a propagator of unyielding unforgivingness. Unforgivingness, is a crippling infection that renders us spiritually handicapped as the poison of bitterness saturates and separates us from the one who loves and cares for us the most.

Without my father there, my mom raised us alone. Growing up I did not see the inner workings of marriage on a daily basis. A romantic at heart, my romantic notions were stimulated by books and movies. When I married, I expected nothing less than a Hollywood picture-perfect marriage. I thought my husband should perform great romantic gestures. Romance is important in a marriage but I was lost in unrealistic fantasies. When Leslie's actions did not meet my fantasies I thought he was the one who did not understand. I overlooked the love in so many of his gestures. I really thought he did not care enough to fulfill my desires. Every action or lack of action, I had taken so personally.

Growing up I had also become quite independent and I prided myself in being able to take care of myself. Prior to marriage my future looked abstract and full of marvelous options. I was a daydreamer, always envisioning a future with endless challenges and fascination. I pictured myself traveling to many places and meeting all kinds of people. With marriage that vision of my future suddenly got narrower and blurry. It wasn't until after I was married that I asked myself crucial questions: Could I really commit to a vow of love and behold my partner in sickness and in health, until death do us part? Was this really my calling, or had I been caught up in the excitement of our courtship? My options seemed so limited. Resentment and doubt had also come from that loss of independence.

"Thank you God for my answers."

Oh, but he wasn't finished just yet. He let me know my biggest mistake had been in taking my eyes off him. Yes, I went to church regularly but I had doubted God's uniting Leslie and I, and turned inward instead of toward him for guidance. I had given Satan an entry point in which to wreak havoc in my mind. The desire of the devil was to hold me down trapping me into a situation in which I felt defenseless. The adversary's plan is the annihilation of God's children and often times he blindfolds us causing us to live in denial of what is happening to us.

There were many times, especially with the older couple, that God tried to get me to change, but selfishness had taken over. I was not in tune with God's will for my life any more. Selfishness allowed me to consume myself with just my way, my wants, my needs.

I took full responsibility for the answers in so many prayer sessions and stepped forward to answer my call as a servant of God, a mother, and a wife. I set before me the map of reconciliation to follow as a guide to help me mend my nonchalant ways. Satan tempted me to the right and to the left but I was now steadfast in resistance. I made a commitment to submission. Had I not done so, the demons would still continue to lurk under my wings. For so long I yearned for fellowship with my God but the burden had laid me down. In prayer, I took all my burdens and laid them at his feet.

"God." I begged.

"Release me; let me go of the cares of this world. Let me go and let you have your way, please Lord, come in with your strength and your power. Come in your own special way, I need a fresh touch, a fresh anointing. Fill me with new

joy and peace, it will sustain me with whatever trials I'm facing. Lift me up above the storms of life. I have looked down and viewed the storms of life but they are insignificant when seen from my vantage point. Let me stay close to you. If I spend time in fasting and prayer and stay in Your Word I know you will listen and I will hear you when you speak. No longer will I allow the so-called 'strongman' who is Satan to enter my chamber. I claim my authority under your name to sweep him out of my life so he will not be able to have me thinking evil thoughts; self-pity, depression, strife, and discouragements any more. I have the legal rights to declare and to keep my word. Your grace is sufficient to carry me through."

BEYOND MY NEEDS
Chapter 8

The restless unknown longing
Of my searching soul would not cease
Until God came in his glory
and my soul found peace.
Everything that has been
shattered will mend again
For there is absolutely nothing
new beneath the sun
I knew not from whence it came
or whether it will go,
For it's as inexplicable
as the restless winds that blow,
And like the wind this too will pass.

Yes, I'm awakening to the fragrance of the roses
Blooming lavishly before my eyes.
Hills and valleys are revived
As Mother Nature comes alive.
I thank the gracious Lord above
For his precious gift of love.
For with love expressed in effervescent spring
And every vibrant living thing
We can now sing a new song
to make our hearts glad.

The time came to put away the mirror; I held it up for so long. This was the next step to recovery; to look beyond myself.

Now it was time to look beyond my needs and take responsibility for my share of the marriage. I now saw the impact of my life on those around me; there was no turning back. My eyes and heart began to open up beyond my hurts. I began to think more about what my husband's, children's and God's needs were. With newfound faith, I paved a new path before me. I devoted myself to the changes my heart and mind were experiencing. I devoured anything that would help me. I continued prayer, asked for advice, read books, researched as much as I could, and tried my best to put into practice what I learned. The changes were difficult and took time but I was determined.

"Human beings, by changing the inner attitudes of their minds; can change the outer aspects of their lives. As within so without."

Thankfully, God did not frustrate me by showing me all I had to accomplish in one setting. No, for that would only have given me a feeling of hopelessness.

He just unveiled what he wanted me to do one moment at a time. When I achieved one feat, he showed me something else I was capable of doing. His only pre-requisites were for me to be willing and obedient.

INVALUABLE LESSONS
Chapter 9

The lessons I've learned are priceless,
They will not be sold but they must be told.
Their retail value cannot be determined
But their value must be displayed.
No one else can fulfill my part.
This was something I had to do for myself.

The lessons learned from different sources were numerous. I know they were all sent to me by God to help my journey.

Marriage, I was shown with new clarity, is supposed to be a partnership. A true partnership requires compromise. Each person is an individual, with their own temperament, their own ideas and desires. When two persons come together in marriage to form a whole, their individual personalities do not automatically merge effortlessly. Friction and conflict are cold, harsh realities of life. Compromise and cooperation are the keys to enmesh the two into one greater whole.

Early on, I ignored the small differences between Leslie and me. I believed them minor, and that they would go away as time passed. That was not the case, time was a fertilizer. Even in good relationships, small irritants can escalate until friends become foes and family and friends become tolerated enemies. Seemingly minor occurrences just sitting in my mind grew disproportionately bothersome. Eventually, they had become intolerable and unbearable, even though the "injuries" sustained were not life threatening.

I learned life and love would be impossible to survive without coming to terms with some of his habits. He surely came to terms with some of mine. The other issues, I learned to attend to them promptly, before they had a chance to grow. I had to communicate my feelings with my husband in a mature fashion, speaking in a calm manner. No longer could I use derogatory remarks that had severely damaged our love life. I had to be clear and just focus on the matter at hand, not stray into another issue. I had to give Leslie a chance to hear it and respond. For so long, I had demanded my wants alone and disregarded many of Leslie's needs, desires, and points of view. We would need to stop ourselves from falling into old traps, stop dealing with recurring problems the same old way, and really communicate instead of just arguing over the matter. Once an issue is resolved, I must not revisit the past. Past mistakes, disappointments, and disagreements brought back up, can produce a lot of stress. They can also cause history to repeat itself or make a current situation more explosive than it really is.

Put into practice, Leslie and I have had to get pretty creative many times in order to reach a middle ground that worked for both of us. Creative compromises helped a great deal in allowing us to stick to our agreements better. A sense of humor also helped us solve problems and come to terms with our individual differences.

I also came to realize that if God made man and woman to act the same way it would be a boring relationship. Leslie and I are two different genders that God created in his own image and likeness; this makes me acknowledge the goodness of God.

I did some research and found out that, in fact, the way we had problems communicating with each other for years was partly biological. There are gender disparities in brain chemistry structure and activity. In other words, men and women really do think and communicate differently. Also, by nature, women are more emotional. This makes us more sensitive than men and even outright needy at times.

One of the most encouraging discoveries I came across was that the gender gap in our brain function narrows as we age. As we get older, we get to understand each other better and become more alike. Reading that information gave me even more hope for the future of my marriage.

Even better, we can help condition the mind and make the process go faster. We can be more conscious of our thoughts and redirect them. It takes a strong will but eventually, the mind molds itself to the new thoughts and behaviors. Add God's guidance and will to that and great changes occur, as began to happen with me. I started consciously reordering my thoughts and allowed God to guide me.

Even reordering my thinking, the natural process could have taken years. But in the spiritual world, I did not have to wait years and years to fulfill the call God placed on my life. There is no limit to how fast we can grow up spiritually and there is no limit to how high we can grow spiritually. There is no sure thing as "arriving" spiritually; as long as we are on this earth we can always get better and better.

"Love dies only when growth stops."

A born again believer, who sets his eyes on God, is determined to be like him and who never turns back, can quickly surpass a person who simply has been plodding along for years. I now rejoice that I am single-minded in serving the Lord.

This was an amazing concept for me, not only could I actively change my marriage, it could get increasingly better. Remaining stationary, would have meant stagnation; I continued my efforts and moved forward.

"You'll never make it," said some people; who had witnessed the years of my marital distress and had the audacity to say it to my face when they heard of my efforts. They even thought they were right. Regardless, I held no grudge for them. They had no knowledge of what

God had planned for Leslie and me. They might have thought they were doing the right thing and looking out for my best interest but they were unaware of the work God was doing in my marriage. I just went ahead and continued with my efforts in the fulfillment of God's plan.

I kept plodding onward hoping I might prove them wrong. They even shook their heads in wonder that I lacked the sense to quit. I held my chin up higher and did not mind a bit. They said I would never make it because of how the problems had multiplied; yet I had to make the effort and try to the best of my ability. So I dug my heels in deeper. Sometimes my spirit lagged; I shouldered what was lightest and the rest I sort of dragged. At the end of the day, to my amazement, I found that what they said was not possible I managed anyway. All it took was three little words; Lord help me.

Memories of how we two lovers came together in the first place allowed me to find more reasons to stay with my husband. God had not erred in bringing us together; we were not meant to go through life without one another. I saw how the bondage I carried for years had prevented me from enjoying the magnitude of love God had divined upon us.

As time went by, countless changes took place in me. My perspective changed radically. The vow I made to love and to hold, in sickness and in health, till death do us part, weren't just words I had uttered, but words I started putting into practice each and everyday. Eventually, I rid myself of doubt and all that the cynics said I would never do, I did.

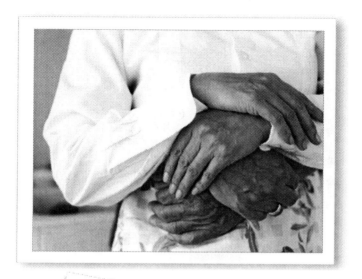

LIFE NOW
Chapter 10

Life now is exquisitely lovely.
Life, a flowing springtime tree
With all of life's branches
Reaching out in perfect symmetry.

Love now proves itself a thousand times a day
In the simplest things we say and do.
It is a thing called sacrifice;
it is a tonic when I am blue.
When there is true love it gives joy to do things
For someone who is dear to you.

The woman I have grown to be is a fervent wife and a sweet and tender mother. I've heard this time and time again and so it must be true. Not only have I become a better wife, I've become a new person from the inside out. The things I used to say and do are no longer a part of me. I no longer have any desire to leave or run away from my marriage. I learned to deal and face up to my responsibilities. I have learned not to hold on to hurt; it's never worth the price it requires. I'm no longer afraid to say I'm sorry when I'm wrong and under no circumstance will I ever retire to bed in wrath. Leslie and I have a bigger and stronger relationship. Life has ultimately been good and without a shadow of a doubt I know that our life will remain as it should; because of the transformation that was wrought within me. The key is that I am now accountable for my part, instead of always blaming someone else.

I know in earlier years those laws of love and kindness I could not have kept. My early aim to win the idle glory of name fades like a candle in the noonday's glow. Oh how I've mourned through bitter tears my loss in sorrow's blindness had fate been less foul? The woman who might abandoned her life to the madness that springs from and ends in despair? As the fire on earth sheds brightness around, neglected many level the walls to the ground. The world makes grave errors in judging these things. Great good and great evil are born in the breast. Love horns, hoofs or gives us our wings and the best could be worst as the worst could be best. I thank God for my own worth, for what I grew to be, for the demons lurked under the angel in me.

The light of Christ now shines in me. His glory I will not share but I will be a true soldier so that men will be prepared. If you struggle in your relationship, you may be walking in darkness but I'm here to show you there is a way. To let you know that God cares. He is concerned about your every need. My motto is "love will conquer." Of course, there are still times when the pressure is on and I feel myself getting weary. But, God truly began a work in me. In those times, I read the Word of God, meditated, and prayed. Out of the abundance of faith in my heart, my mouth speaks words of life, not words of death, words of faith, not words of fear. I'm often reminded of a book I once read. I no longer remember the title or the author but the following is my memory of its inspiration.

You have given much, and much has been required of you. Sometimes it seems that the more you give of yourself, the more people require of you.

As you give, people are not aware of your motives, but God is well aware that you stretch yourself to the utter limits of human endurance, because you want to please him.

Every job you undertake, you do it well. Yes, I know my child, there are many people who are appreciated and rewarded financially who have not toiled the long hours you have. They have not paid the price that you have paid to serve me.

You have given your all and the world has not recognized it. Many have put you on the same level as other people. They have taken you for granted but I have not. I see and I know what goes into the final product and you shall have your reward. You are doing what I called you to do and I shall repay you. Your harvest is at hand. Never fail to turn to me in your hour of despair, never fail to turn to me in your hour of joy. I want you to come to me with every thought you have, every problem you have, every joy you have. I am interested in you. I love you, come to me and your life will be fulfilled. In me you will find life and life more abundant.

Through me your mistakes can be turned around for your good. I am a forgiving Father, I don't want you to live in the past and dwell on your failures. No, my child, that is not my desire for you. My desire is that you climb higher and higher in me. When you make a mistake, all you have to do is repent. Pick yourself up and keep on moving in my direction. Never fail to turn to me, with every problem you have, every question, I am interested. As long as you are in the world, storms will come into your life, but you are not to be tossed to and fro by the storms. There is no storm that can overcome you when you remember to call upon me. Use my Name and my Word."

ROMANCE
Chapter 11

But ever following each magnet
My sad repining heart was met
with unexpected pleasure.
I thought it only happened so
But this has taught me,
no least thing from my life can go.
But something else is brought me, it is the law,
Complete sublime and now with unshaken faith in
Patience I but bide my time when any joy is taken no
Matter if the crushing blow
may for the moment drown me.
Still back of it waits love I know for a fact, with some
Now gift to crown me. All we bestow on causes of me
Love or hate of malice on devotion somehow,
Sometimes shall be returned again.
There is no wasted toil, no lost emotion.
The motto of the world is "give and take"
It gives favors out of sheer good will but unless
Speedy response or recompense is made,
You'll find yourself presented with its bill.

After everything Leslie and I have been through, we have recaptured the romance. And, after more than twenty years of marriage, fallen in love all over again countless times. Frequently, Leslie will buy me a bouquet of flowers. He compliments me on the least thing I do around the house, especially when I cook his favorite meal. These are proof my mate still cares for me.

He had yearned for greater closeness and romance but I did not recognize it before. As I began to see his needs for romance, I began bringing him into the fireplace of my heart so much until he could hardly stand it. I watched him blush many times as I grabbed him in my arms and held him so tight he had no way to escape. It felt good; that is what I needed to have done all this time. Knowing what it's like to come home from a hard day's labor, I would wait up to receive him in the warmth of my fireplace as soon as he entered the door. He must have felt the heat because it knocked him off his feet. Romantic, loving gestures like these helped reignite our love. They have also kept the embers glowing.

I don't think Leslie minds the fact that his wife is sensual, but you see, I don't allow my sensuality to interfere with my spirituality. I aim to please my man. But make no mistake; I always aim to please my God. This is what gives us the desire and the commitment to each other even after 20-years of marriage.

Keeping up romantic acts like these in my marriage is one of the quirks that makes me who I really am, who I wanted to be for so long. But, oh boy, is it challenging to keep up. Pedicures, manicures, bubble baths, massages, and more. The wining and dining in candlelight occasionally, is pretty easy but all others are a constant effort.

Achieving the level of romance we have now is one thing, maintaining it is another. Sometimes it seems a bit much but it comes with the new package. Some women do these and much more for their man each day, so why shouldn't I? The results however are worth all the work.

"For it is only in giving and sharing
in the heart's delight that we receive."

Leslie was dressed for church one Sunday morning as I deliberately approached him in our bedroom.

"The smell of your perfume makes me wild," I said. "And if I may say, man, I love your profile."

We almost didn't make it to church.

I definitely have a new attitude. My husband never knows what ideas his wife will be coming up with next. He knows I will surprise him in areas he never dreamed of.

Once, as we were lying in bed, I began reading him a poem from Songs of Solomon, from my favorite book; the Bible.

> *"I'm black but comely. Kiss me, I said, with the kisses of your mouth, for thy love is better than wine."*

He was amazed.

> *"Tell me, O thou whom I loveth, where thou makes thy flock to rest. For why should I be the one that turneth aside by flocks of thy companions?"*

He was enthused.

"Tell me, O thou whom I loveth, thou fairest among men, I have compared you to a company of horses in pharaoh's chariots. While the king sitteth at his table, my spikenard sendeth for the smell thereof a bundle of myrrh is my well beloved. Unto me he shall lie all night betwixt my breast."

He was stunned.

"Thou art fair my love. Thou art fairer and have dove's eyes. I am the apple of thy heart and sit under your shadow with great delight as fruit so sweet to your taste. Stay with me, comfort me with apples for I am sick of love, please let your left hand stay under my head..."

He complied. Before he could interrupt, I continued,

"...and let your right hand embrace me. I charge you Oh my beloved by the hinds of the field that ye stir not up nor awake my love 'til he please."

He turned in anticipation.

"Thy lips are like a thread of scarlet. Thy neck, mm, mm, is like the tower of David. Thy hands are as pillars of marble set upon sockets of fine gold. How fair is thy love my brother, my spouse. How much better is thy love than wine. And the smell of thine ointment that all spices. Thy lips o my spouse,"

He licked his lips like a cat that drinks the last drop of milk.

"Drops as the honeycomb, honey and milk are under thy tongue, the smell of thy garment is like the smell of Lebanon, a garden enclosed is my brother, my spouse. A spring shut up, a fountain sealed. Awake, Oh north wind and come south blow upon my garden that she spices thereof may flow out. Let my beloved come into his garden and eat his pleasant fruits. I am my beloved's and his desire is toward me. Many waters cannot quench love, neither can the floods drown it. If a man would give all the substance of his house for love, it would utterly be contemned."

My husband and I do not take each other for granted anymore. Instead of falling straight to sleep, we thank God for each other; and for the pleasures it gives us when we make love. It is so nice to love and to be loved. Love is beautiful and meant to be shared; not hidden away from sight.

Happy is the heart that beats with love. God has born our hearts to him by unnumbered tokens in heaven and in earth. Though the things of nature and the deepest and tenderest earthly ties that human hearts can know. He has sought to reveal himself to us, although imperfectly, yet these represent his love. Though all the evidence has been given, the enemy of God blinded the minds of men so that they looked upon God with fear; they thought of him as severe and unforgiving. How can we not contemplate on the amazing love of God and the sacrifice he made to give up the only son he has; to claim the loss, and to bring them back to him. None other than the son of God could have accomplished the mission for salvation. It is only he who was in the bosom of the Father could have declared him, and only he who knew the height and depth of the love of God could make it manifest. Nothing less than the infinite sacrifice of love made by our Lord on behalf of the fallen race, could have expressed the fathers love for humanity. God so loved the world that he gave, and with the example he showed; you must likewise follow in his footsteps and love one another. The mysteries of love are not easy to comprehend. We all might have some *"...knowledge and faith, so much so that we could move mountains but if there is no love it profiteth nothing. Though I bestow all my goods to feed the poor, give my body to be burned, and have not loved, it profiteth me nothing. Love suffereth long and is kind, envieth not, vaunteth not, is not puffed up, does not behave itself unseemly. Seeketh not her own, nor is love easily provoked, or thinketh evil. Love rejoiceth not in iniquity but rejoiceth in the truth, love beareth all things, believeth all things, hopes and endureth all things, it never faileth: now abideth faith and hope but the greatest and most important one of these is love."* 1 Corinthians 13.

FINAL THOUGHTS
Chapter 12

True love is hard to bend
And will never break
If we give everything within.
In every dark cloud above,
One will see a silver lining
Blazing through the stars
To light the years,
The heart, and rebirth God's
Promise of eternal life.

As I summarized in its entirety the situations that almost destroyed my own marriage, it reaffirms my faith wholeheartedly. The ultimate example of The Master's embrace and presence was our healing. And when it seems that any movement will disfigure the design, he rearranges life like a moved kaleidoscope.

Many times the vows we make before God are broken so easily. Marriage today has a bad rap, and in the midst of marital troubles, some of us even forget that God made that union. Yet, they thought so at the time they said, "I do." The two who in each other made joy out of living, sometimes watch their gladness fade. All too often we fall passionately in love, then distrust and rage at each other. Regardless of the severity of the situation, it is our duty to try our best to keep the promises we made in front of, and to, him. After all, God's desire is for us to experience life's pleasures in love on his holiest level.

His love will work in ways that are wondrous and strange. There is nothing in life that love cannot change. Love transforms into the most common places. It transforms into beauty, splendor, grace and sweetness. Love is unselfish, understanding, and not with the mind. It is also the answer that we seek for so long; The language that speaks. We cannot buy it because it is priceless and free.

God never takes one thing away from us but has always been giving to us. Straight through my heart this fact today by truth's own hand is driven. So much drama can be avoided if we just think about what Jesus would do, and would want us to do, in the same situation. It will enable us to open our spiritual eyes to see what is going on around our lives. Most importantly, if God be in all our doings, we can be "overcomers." We can grow apart in a marriage, but it can be traced to how conflicts are resolved. The situation does not have to become fatal or final if we are more tolerant and willing to work out our problems with an open heart. No matter what the circumstance may be in life, God is able to see us through. He will even go to extremes, if the problems seem too hard and you don't know what to do. If life seems empty and everything around looks gray and not blue, there is someone who cares for you.

I have had to console myself in God on many days when I felt down and out. There has always been a song a word or a poem that I can read to lift me up. I love being reminded of the words of one of my favorite poems taken from the book *Love Letters from God: Affirmations for your Soul* by Bonnie G. Schluter. I am sure this will also be of blessing to you:

"*His eyes are on the sparrow and he watches over thee, so much how ye of little faith. He has watched you sow seeds of love in rocky fields, you have tilled the soil in the lives of many. You have removed the rocks, the hurts, the pain, etc and you are not even aware of all you do. But my child, you do it so effortlessly that your __ is yours. Others may want to be like you but they don't know how. Yet, just your presence helps people. You have underestimated your God given abilities because of low self-esteem but my child, it's time for you to arise. Yes, I know there are times when you do feel joyful but you really aren't aware of the effect your presence has on other people. You became so much apart of their lives that they cannot even comprehend how dull and lifeless their lives would be without.*

You are a source of peace; you are a source of joy, comfort and patience. You are that beautiful branch that draws from the vine. Can't you see my child how much you contribute to society and to the well-being and happiness of others? That is why I am telling you today you are a very special part of the body of Christ and thought the enemy comes against you in all direction, fear not my child I am with you."

Words like these remind me that this old road will lead me home. Though I stumbled on the way, there was and still is hope for tomorrow. That continues as strength for me today. It was the hand of God that drew back the curtain of time to let me see his mighty hand at work and allow me to get an inkling of what awaits in his eternity. Those years of searching and longing are faint memories: I am free! The glory of that movement still enfolds me, though now it's gone beyond my earthly sight. I know God lives and there is a glorious future. I am glad for the experience of watching his healing in such a miraculous way.

After spending fifteen months patching up wounded men on Europe's battlefields, Joseph Portnoy, a

World War II veteran, packed away his army uniform and bronze star. He came home to his wife and as he held her in his arms he quoted:

> "Ask God to give you what you want. Help Him to justify your wants by the way that you live and then, having given Him your prayer, have the faith and courage to rely on His power to do the things that are right in His eyes."

But as I continued to read this article I realized that he had written to her before coming home and in his letter Portnoy also quoted:

> "God had little to do with the war; wars will go on as long as men's hearts are as they are."

This really took a hold on me and as I gave it my deepest thought; I thanked God that he has allowed me a change of heart. Yes the war will go on in our hearts and life if we refuse to make peace with our fellow men. This is what God had intended for us but because of sin, we have to live in war with each other.

"But there is a way that seemeth right."

We are God's precious jewels. If we just love each other and try our best to live peaceably with all men, beginning with our own family, we can fulfill the will of God in our lives. And the seeds God planted in our lives can grow and get fully grown, ready to bear much fruit so that everyone we come in contact with can take and eat of the same spirit. With the spirit of joy, peace, patience, gentleness, goodness, faith, meekness, humility and temperance we can rise to any storm that should come upon us. When storms of life come, they bring with them forces that easily over power our human resources and comprehension. Homes and material and our belongings are sometimes ravished, destroyed, and washed away, leaving people with just the clothes on their backs. Storms also bring revelations, reveal the heart of people, their courage and compassion or their selfishness and greed.

But on a spiritual level, storms represent cleansing. When storms leave lives in tatters that have to be rebuilt, it requires mental and emotional letting go of the old possessions and the past; and forces us to look inward and upward to begin again.

Rebuilding requires tapping into an inner strength to accomplish that which seems impossible. When we are cognizant of the divine presence within us and around us, we can be marveled at how God makes a way out of no way and glorious order and sunshine returns.

So with deeper joys of which I dreamed,
Life yields more rapture than did childhood fancies;
And each year brings more pleasure than I waited.
Friendship proves truer than all it seemed,
And beyond youth's passion hued romances;
Love is more perfect than anticipated.

Printed in the United States
80495LV00001B/493-639